Uncovered

Uncovered

Uncovered

Kee'Twana Williams

Pen2Pad Ink
Publishing

Uncovered

ISBN: 978-1-970135-83-1 Paperback
       978-1-970135-84-8 Ebook

Published in the United States by Pen2Pad Ink Publishing.

Requests to publish work from this book or to contact the author should be sent to: keetwana.williams@gmail.com

Kee'Twana Williams retains the rights to all images.

Uncovered

I dedicate this book to every boy, girl, man, and woman who has experienced sexual abuse at any level, to every voiceless victim, and to every silent tear cried. It is NOT your fault.

Uncovered

Acknowledgements

I want to thank the Lord for choosing me and never leaving. I want to thank every person that played a role in my story. To the people who molested me I forgave you years ago, because if I didn't, I would be stuck in a place that was too dark to live.

Thank you to my friends Rachel, Nikki and Lae-Triana, meeting you guys my sophomore year of college kept me alive.

Thank you to my Delta Beta Sisters for completely changing my college experience and letting me know that the authentic me is loveable.

Thank you to my First Lady A'Besa Hodge for always being a listening ear and pushing me to open-up when I needed to.

Lastly, I would like to say thank you to thank the people I offended for hearing me and forgiving me, without that I don't think I would have been able to write this book.

Uncovered

Preface

When I look at pictures of myself from the early 2000s, I can tell that girl was so lost. She didn't know who she was. She found her identity in what she did and her worth in the people she hung around. She needed to have colored hair. It needed to be straight, her eyes had to be colored, she had to have contacts, and she never wore glasses. She wasn't just lost. She was the dangerous type of lost where she didn't know she was lost. She thought she was living this good ol' Christian life with just a dash of sin. In actuality, she was living a life, drowning in sin, with a dash of Christianity.

I felt like I was striving to do my best when I didn't know who I was. So, my best was the worst for me. I didn't know who I was, so I didn't really grasp who I belonged to. I didn't think about the fact that Jesus died just for me. He paid the price for my life. If I was the only person on this earth, He would have still died for me alone. So, I lived as this person with a cover over myself. I didn't just wear a mask. I had an armor that fully covered me. I never let anyone in enough to take the armor off because I wasn't sure if I existed underneath it. It's like when people sit in their bed for years, and their legs don't really work anymore. That was the struggle of my life. I had lived in that armor so long that my mind didn't know how to function outside of the armor. So, I had to ask myself: How do I live an UNCOVERED life with God? What does that even mean? I didn't discover that until this book. So, I ask that you pray with me and not prey on me while reading this book. God has called me to be UNCOVERED in this season.

It Happened

I saw a picture on Facebook of a sad little girl in the back seat of a car and the mother was driving. She asked "What's wrong? You haven't been the same since you left your cousin's house." The post then revealed the back story of her being molested by her cousin. This image brought me to tears. I realized this little girl was very similar to me. As much as I tried to forget that IT HAPPENED, I could not hold back the emotions. The memories and emotions came rushing back to me as if I was in the moment.

Fourth grade. Most are concerned about multiplying double digits. Putting letters together to create new vocabulary words. Not getting caught during recess tag games. Me? I was trying to avoid a penis being shoved down my throat by my cousin. He forced me to perform oral sex on multiple occasions. Other cousins and family members could play outside. He held me back and made me get on my knees. Empty bedrooms. Bathrooms. Closets. It happened in multiple places, but it was always behind a closed door just in case someone tried to walk in. Oddly enough, it always happened when others were around, so to me it felt like a secret that wasn't such a secret. How is nobody noticing us missing together so much?

Nobody ever thought twice about it. Anytime I saw him, I was on my knees. He became a coach: telling me what to do and what not to do with this great "skill". According to him, "I love you. This is what you do for those you love." Rape turned into an expression of love in my eyes. It didn't hurt me, and it made him feel better so nothing seemed wrong to me. With all the attention, I began to cling to him. Before I knew it, the molestation became the norm for me.

These moments changed the trajectory of my life in a mighty way. My sexuality was a wrapped gift. He peeled the ribbon, undid the tape, and took the wrapping paper off very slowly. I didn't know what to do with it now that it was unwrapped. I was also frustrated with the fact that I did not know how to deal with the response my body was having to the rape.

My curiosity about sexual activity was ignited. I knew sex was wrong. No one should touch my private area because that's what I was taught. However, oral sex was not something I ever remember talking about with my parents, at school, or with anyone at all. I had no clue what to do with all these feelings I was having. There was so much going on in my mind and my body at such a young age. It made me feel uncomfortable. My eyes were always wandering and examining the crotches of men. I was so curious about all things concerning sex.

I felt horrible about this feeling. These thoughts made me feel "fast" or "hot" as the old people would say. Some of my family members would call me those things all the time. Sometimes, it made me feel like I did something to make him molest me. I thought if my family is saying these things about me then I must be portraying something that invited him to molest me. Because of this, no one could know about it. This would forever be a secret between us.

Before I entered the 6th grade, the consistent molestation had stopped. I would always think if I could just remember the first time it happened then I could figure out why it happened. I still don't have the memory of the first time, but I remember very clearly the last time it was supposed to happen.

I went behind a door or into a bathroom every time I saw him. I went into the bathroom and waited with the lights off. I waited for a while and no one came in. I walked out and made eye contact with him, and he gave me a "do not worry about it" type of signal. I was confused. I never had that response before. I didn't know if there were too many people around or if I did something wrong or if it was over. So, I just went outside and played. It never happened again. We just went back to normal as if nothing happened. We continued to be a "normal" family, and no one ever knew what happened between us.

Playing House Gone Wrong

The game of "Playing House" is a staple in the lives of most children who grew up before cellular devices and with a lot of family members who were baby sat by the same elderly family member. We all know how it works: Someone plays mom. Someone plays dad. Everyone else plays the children. If you didn't have real family members, girls usually used their dolls. It didn't matter if they were Cabbage Patch or Barbie. A doll is a doll.

I was that doll for a new family member. He "played house" with me all the time. He would kiss and rub on me. According to him, "That's what parents do". I went along with it because I was familiar with how family loves each other and maybe this was just a new way of expressing it. I did realize, however, that being groped and massaged was not right. I knew sex was bad, so I knew that was not something I should be doing with anyone let alone a family member. I constantly had to tell him "no" and "stop". Anytime there was a silent moment or a dark space, he would try. So I began to lay on my stomach so that my private area was harder to reach.

There was one occasion I was laying down watching television. He came in the room and just laid right on top of me and started humping me. I didn't pay him any attention. I just continued to watch the television. He pulled the back of my pants down and tried to have sex with me. He tried for a little while to have sex with me, but I kept quietly pushing him off me. I didn't want this person to get in trouble or not talk to me anymore, so I didn't fight much. I remember being so scared that day. I thought something bad was going to happen, and that I wouldn't be able to see my family anymore. I never said anything about the situation to anyone. Like my earlier molester, I started to cling to this person as well. Eventually, he stopped and we pretended like nothing ever happened.

My enrollment in a sex education class taught me that these incidents were not acts of love. Simultaneously, I couldn't tell anyone. I started to blame myself. Why were these men always choosing me? What did I do to make them feel like this was okay? Pieces of my self-worth and value were slowly ripped away from me. I was just a rag doll being tossed to and fro with no true owner who cared for me. Just when I thought things were getting close to normal, I learned that friends also saw me as another doll for their game of playing house.

All the neighborhood kids were chilling at my homeboy's house which was nothing unusual for us. Everyone was in the backyard. "I'm going to the restroom." I told everyone.

"Wait! Let me come with you. I have new posters" he said. Back then, I was obsessed with posters of singers and rappers. My walls were covered with them at my house. I went into his room, and he showed me the poster. As I was getting ready to walk out, he ran to the door and shut it.

"Dude. Quit playing. I'm trying to go back outside." I told him. He locked the door. I reached for the knob. He pushed me back towards the bed. He pinned my hands down with one arm and with his other hand he began to pull up my shirt and pull down my bra. I was kicking and screaming for help, but everyone was outside. He straddled me, starting kissing on me, and began to pull down my pants. I began to kick even harder to the point he couldn't get my pants down, so he began to rip them off. They ripped down the side, and he lost his grip on me. So, I was able to kick him, get loose, and run out of the house.

I ran back to my granny's house. I cried so hard the whole time I was running. He only lived a block away from my granny's house, but that was the longest run of my life. I was trying to take it all in and think of what I was going to say to my granny, because I didn't want him to get in trouble. When I got to the door I stopped, calmed myself, and got myself together. To my surprise my grandmother was sitting in the living room wide awake.

"What's wrong baby?" She asked.

"Nothing." I said sniffling.

"Well, what happened to your pants?" She replied. A river of tears started to flow from my eyes.

"Well...I...I was going to the restroom, and he wanted me to see some posters in his room.... When...I went to his room...he...he tried to have sex with me...He ripped my pants tryin' to get them off! What am I going to do, Granny?!" She sat next to me and started hugging me.

"It's ok...It's ok, baby...Let it out..." She said softly. I was grateful for her warm touch even in this hot weather. I looked down at my pants.

"What am I going to do about my pants?!" I asked through broken sobs. She looked down. "Can you fix them?" I asked.

"Uh...let's get you into some new pants. Then, we can call the police and talk to them--"

"Wait!" I interrupted. "No! I don't want them to know. I don't want Mama to know either...I...I don't want anyone to get in trouble." She nodded her head, took the pants, and I went off to bed...

The next day, I was waiting for my mom to pick me up. My grandmother came into the room. "Sweetie, Sit down" she said. She took my hand and exhaled before she started speaking.

"I...I'm going to tell your mom. This is not something I can be comfortable with keeping away from her." My eyes widened.

"No! She's gonna blow this out of proportion! I don't...I don't wanna get anyone in trouble, Granny!" I exclaimed.

"But if you don't say something, he may do this to someone else! That's not right!"

"But this..." I started to tell her that this wasn't my first experience with men I love trying to rape me, but I decided to keep my mouth close. "I just...I don't wanna deal with this!" I said instead. When my mom arrived, she told her what happened. My mom was furious! My dad was enraged. I was more afraid of what they would do to my ex-homeboy than the police! Still, I ended up telling the police what happened. He was put on house arrest, but I never stepped foot in that house again.

Passing on The Unwanted Gift

Regifting: the art of taking something you have received and giving it to someone else. It is always something you didn't want. It is usually something you will never use. I can't say the same. I will admit. This part of my testimony is the hardest. It also makes me angry. It's hard because of what I have done, but I'm angry because I am certain I am not the only person who has experienced this.

One of my friends told me that "A lot of sexual abuse victims feel shame, but they fail to realize that shame is when you feel bad for who you were taught to be. It's not who you are. It's not where you need to stay." That friend was correct. When these horrible experiences happen in our lives, we protect the predator because they are a part of our family. That family member is never exposed, but we are. We become known as "fast" or "hot". We internalized those stereotypical labels to the point where they become our truth. Everything is our fault, and we need to fix the problem.

What is our solution? Some of us change our sexual interest.

We switched from liking males to females in hopes of quelling the stereotype and moving forward with our lives. Unfortunately, that doesn't work either. We get ridiculed for being a lesbian! So here we are: wrong for being sexually active at a young age, wrong for being "fast" or "hot", and wrong for liking girls. All of these "wrongs" start to pile on us like we are carrying bags of boulders. It is heavy. It is painful. And we suffer in silence. For some us eventually we knowingly or unknowingly introduce other people or family members to the same experiences. This cycle continues for generations and generations... and I'm sad to say that I was a part of keeping that cycle alive.

I heard someone say that "Bad habits are hard to break". I believed them for a long time. My belief of love was clouded by the sexual events that took place when I was at such a young age. I didn't really have an effective example of what love should really be, so I started to express love the only way I knew how.

I showed some family members what love looked like in a family by introducing them to oral sex. I went from being the victim to the offender. (Whew! That's a hard sentence to type. It is the most shameful thing to me that I have done in my whole life.) I showed to them what I was being told to do by those family members who molested and raped me. At the time, I didn't know what molestation was or that it was even happening to me. I just thought this was a different way to express love to family. I don't recall how long this went on or how many times it happened.

It would happen at night before we went to sleep. At some point, it stopped when I realized that this was not the definition of love, and it was not supposed to have happened to me either. I felt embarrassed that I did that to anyone, especially my family. I felt shameful, disgusting, and nasty. I felt as if I didn't deserve to have any feelings about what I experienced because I had done it to other people.

Once we stopped, we just went on as if nothing was wrong. We went back to being a "normal" family. But there was nothing normal about it. Since no one told us differently, we went on doing what we were taught: Family is everything. Love your family, have their backs, and protect your family. My family is not the only one that follows this creed. It is kind of a typical statement spoken in most Black families.

Letting people into your "house" or your "business" was a HELL NO...no matter how detrimental the situation was to those in the family.

Protecting my predators became the right thing to do, especially since I needed to protect myself. So, I had to find a way to deal with my shame and the molestation. How could I possibly think anyone would care to listen to me after they knew I did the same thing to someone else? I didn't feel I had a right to outcry behind what happened to me, so I just shut all emotions down. I closed my mind to the situation and did my best to forget that it ever happened. If I got sad, I would tell myself, "How dare you!? You don't have the right! Suck it up and get over it!"

From my experience the reason this cycle continues is because of this: A girl is being touched or raped by an older family member. That family member says don't say anything. The girl complies because she loves that family member and doesn't want anything bad to happen to them. For many years, I succeeded in forgetting...I had a very stressful couple of elementary and junior high years. But little did I know these incidents were going to be the root of some issues in my life. As much as I tried to forget about them and clean my memory of them, the residue was everlasting.

Leaving Residue

You come out of a session of taking a bath feeling refreshed. The tub has all your dirt and grime. Leaving that dirt and grime on the tub for long periods of time makes it more difficult to clean and go away. That's how I felt about my life. I tried so hard to wash away all the traumatic experiences with molestation, but they were too hard and too grimy to get rid of.

I thought the pain was gone, but the residue remained. I dealt with the fact that I was molested, but there were more chains attached to these events than I wanted to admit. These events changed me and the things I was interested in.

I had blocked the passing on the unwanted gift part of my story out of my life to the point where I cannot remember much about my childhood. In turn, I lost years of childhood memories. It always bothered me growing up when I saw someone who knew me when I was younger, and I couldn't remember who they were.

I was perverted and promiscuous. I would look at boys' crotches and girls' breasts all the time. I had a strange curiosity about sex at a young age. At times, I felt nasty and guilty that I had all these thoughts, questions, and emotions that I couldn't talk to anyone about. I wanted to watch all the sex scenes in the movies so I could learn more about sex and what it was. My mama was not having that, so I had to find other sources.

This was the beginning of pornography and masturbation taking over my life. I was embarrassed to talk about it, but at the same time I didn't think it was hurting anyone so it wasn't that bad. These are two topics that are not talked about in the church much because they are secret sins, and people like to keep them that way. Some people are too embarrassed to talk about them and some people don't even think they are a sin. I was a person in the middle of those two options.

I started watching porn in sixth grade. Watching porn helped me with my urges that I was feeling. It also made me more curious about sex though. I was too scared to try it, but at the same time, I wanted to know all about it. I would rush home from school so that I could watch porn before my parents got home. I can remember friends asking me to come over to their house after school, and I told them I would come over later because I felt like I had to watch it. Watching porn gave me ideas about how to ease the urges, so I started experimenting with masturbation as well.

My addiction continued into high school. I watched it sometimes to deal with my urges, but other times I just watched it because it was interesting. Porn became like a regular movie to me. I didn't have to be masturbating to watch porn. It was like watching cartoons to me. As I got older, it became available via the internet. Porn saturated my mind because I watched it so much. I remember being upset on days that I couldn't watch it because this was my way of coping with what happened to me. It helped me to answer questions I could not ask others. It helped quell my curiosity.

These two addictions became my best friends, my way out, and my happy place. Anytime I didn't want to feel something, or I wanted to forget about a situation I would turn to porn and masturbation and all would be good after that. Those were really my safe places in my adolescent years and even into adulthood.

This addiction went on from sixth grade through my late twenties. It was not an easy addiction to break. Nobody talked about it and the ones who are, encourage it. Church. Porn. Masturbate. Repeat. It was routine.

I thought for the longest that self-pleasure was better than having sex. I also convinced myself that it was not a sin because I was alone. When I realized that masturbation was not right, I tried my best to stop. Unfortunately, it was not easy at all. My body had been trained for almost 20 years to deal with my urges in this manner.

My soul was crying out to be saved and released from this addiction, but my flesh was enjoying itself too much. I eventually tried to slow down on watching porn. Instead of every day, I would try to only watch a couple of days a week. I knew it wouldn't be easy because I had been watching it for most of my life at this point. I also was in college with a roommate, so it wasn't easy finding time to watch in secret. It didn't stop me, but it did slow me down.

Sex Addiction for Happiness

I stayed a virgin longer than most of my friends at the time. I didn't want to have sex because I felt like I would get addicted. That is exactly what happened. I was never one of those little girls who dreamed about her wedding or her future family. I fantasized about sex: What it would feel like and how my body would react to it. That's what kept me a virgin for so long. I didn't want to try because I feared what I would turn into.

My sexual activity was a power move. I wanted every ounce of strength that was taken from me by family members. In my head, it was my way of regaining value and worth. Feelings never existed. Emotions were nowhere to be found. It was a transaction: get in, get sexually satisfied, get out. I had sex then got up and left until the next time I chose them. It gave me a sense of validation that I am powerful. I am alive and not invisible. It became my new safe place.

My sexual activity was the interstate exit I waited for years and years to finally get to after starting the drive down the road of fornication, abuse, and abandonment. It consumed my mind and my world. It was all I thought about when I went to see my boyfriend. I tried to figure out when and where we could have sex. It was my drug of choice, and I needed it. Anytime my mood was off or I was having a bad day, I would go see my boyfriend. I could escape into the sex world where real life problems didn't exist, nothing in the past affected me, and I didn't have any triggers that reminded of what was done to me or what I had done.

It made all the suppressed emotions take a deep dive back down when they would surface. It melted the sadness of depression away for a moment, but it couldn't take away the depression. Sex numbed me so that I felt nothing but that person touching me. Sex was an escape for me. It was a place where nothing but good things happened. It was my escape from the real world. Sex was about the feeling of escaping reality and going into a world where pain didn't exist. There was no past, no hurt, or no trials. It was simply fun and pleasure. Sometimes, I feared the end. Emotions would come rushing back. I fought back rivers of tears. The temporary fix had its defects, but I still wanted those short seconds where I was free.

I also felt loved, special, and relaxed. Sex became number one in my heart. It was what mattered to me the most. I didn't go to God when I was having a bad day, feeling depressed, or unworthy. I let sex be the answer every single time. I never prayed for any healing. I just needed my boyfriend to answer his phone. If he didn't answer, the side dude was the next choice. All hell broke loose if no one answered. If no one was available, I went back to masturbation. I had zero self-respect and my self-confidence was a non-factor because it was so depleted. Sex overtook my life and was trying to choke the life out of me. I needed to feel better. I was not going to be able to make it through the night with how I was feeling, so I needed to escape from it all.

My mind was always so cluttered, clouded, and full because I had so many areas in my brain that were untouchable due to trauma. I locked lots of traumatic events up in my brain. Anytime I came to that roadblock, I would have to detour to sex to escape the pain. Some people like sex, but for me it was not a choice. I could not get out of a bad mood without having sex. If anyone was around me when I couldn't have sex, I was not pleasant to be around at all. Sex was the greatest high of life. At that time for me sex was the highest point of happiness that I could obtain.

Abortion by Default

I got pregnant my first-time having sex, and I didn't find out until I was almost two months pregnant. I didn't believe this was happening to me! How could it happen? This type of stuff only happens in movies, right? Well, that's what I thought, but this was real life. I missed my period in June, and I thought it was just changing to the beginning of the month. Then July came, and I still had no period.

I was in Houston at the time, and I had to sneak off to buy a pregnancy test. I took the test, and it was "negative" (Honestly...I'm still confused about the test I took). I bought like five more pregnancy tests just to make sure I was not pregnant. They were all negative!! So, I was like *okay my body is doing something stupid, I guess*.

I was on my way back home from Houston, and we stopped at Taco Cabana to get some food. I had a little bit of nachos and a sip of soda, and my stomach was not feeling it. I walked swiftly to the restroom to not cause too much attention, and I threw up. It never dawned on me that I could be pregnant. I had only thrown up one time before that, and it was when I ate Taco Cabana. I figured that it was just the restaurant. When I finally made it back home to Arlington, I threw all the pregnancy tests in the dumpster of our apartment. I had kept them in my bag because I didn't want anyone to know in Houston, so I couldn't throw them in the trash can there.

I got home at night. The very next day, my mama cornered me in my room.

"You pregnant?" she asked sternly.

"NO!" I exclaimed.

"Ok...we gone see."

She took me to the clinic to get a pregnancy test, but I had no worries. I took like five tests, so I was convinced I was not pregnant. The clinic was taking too long, and my mama was over waiting. We ended up buying more store pregnancy tests for me to take.

After I took the test, I went back to my room. There was no need to wait to see this negative result I had seen so many times. Until...

"KeeTwana! Get in here! NOW!" My mama screamed. I ran back to the restroom. When I got there, she was looking down at the pregnancy test like I was in trouble.

"What does that say?" Mama asked.

I looked down. PREGNANT. PREGNANT? PREGNANT. PREGNANT! I was in complete shock. My mother's voice creaked like nails on a chalkboard as she started wailing. I heard pain. I heard anger, but the worst thing I heard in her cry was disappointment. My aunt came over to console her, but her tears of pain hurt my soul. I went to my room and cried mostly from being in shock. Then, I sobbed because I was pregnant. I was 17! What was I going to do with a baby? It's my senior year. How would that work? I had so many questions going through my head. An hour passed and my sobs softened to a whimper. I came to terms with the fact that there was a life. It was inside me. It was growing. It was a beautiful combination of myself and my boyfriend. I was not happy, but I was content.

A couple of days later, I was laying in the bed and my mama came into the room and handed me the phone.

"Hey sweets." My daddy said so lovingly.

"Hey daddy. What's up?" I asked.

"Now, what you gonna do with a baby?"

"Daddy...I don't know. It's not like I planned this." I replied holding back tears.

"You got a lot of life ahead of you. You don't need a baby right now."

"I know, but what am I supposed to do?" I cried out. My mama took the phone back.

"Look. Like your dad said...you have your whole life ahead of you. This isn't that time. You are not ready to take care of a child!" Mama explained.

"Yea...you probably right, but what am I supposed to do about that now? There is a baby in my stomach."

My mother looked at me. "I know exactly what you about to do," she started. "You're going to have an abortion."

My heart sank beneath my body. I felt like all the blood was drained out of my body, and my soul jolted out of me. It was not just from the pain of the word abortion but from the guilt and shame I brought on my parents. I felt like my parents were so embarrassed. There were no words I could say. I turned towards the wall in my bedroom and cried. I couldn't fight or argue with them. Plus, I had nowhere to go or any way to support myself and my child.

90% of me wanted to keep my baby, but that 10% was questioning if it would be worth it. I just knew this baby would make my life meaningful. When I felt a sad emotion, I had sex of some sort and then happiness came. I lived that cycle. This baby was going to be my joy, my problem solver, my purpose, my reason to live, and the source of my happiness. But they were right. I had no way to take care of the child.

"Okay," I started, "I'll...I'll get rid of it."

I will never ever forget the day I went to the abortion clinic. When we pulled up, there were people outside protesting for pro-life. Before I could get out of the car, a woman was walking towards us. The woman who kept telling me "Your baby is a person... it deserves to live... there are resources out there that will help you raise it... keep your baby". That was the longest walk of my entire life. She was very adamant that I should keep this baby, and that made me feel worse about myself. She kept saying "You have a choice", but I didn't feel like I did. Although there was a part of me that didn't want this child, there was a bigger part that did.

The lady walked beside me all the way up to the stairs of the clinic. "Keep your baby. Please...just keep it." She said repeatedly.

When I got inside the clinic, my boyfriend and his mama called me.

"Hello?"

"Baby are you gone do this?" He asked.

"Yes, I am at the clinic" I replied.

"We can keep this baby. Don't go through with this."

"I am already here, and I am going to get an abortion." I muffled out through the tears and silent sobs.

"Kee Kee! You can keep the baby! We will take care of it!" His mother exclaimed.

"How?! How?!" I yelled through swallowed tears, but they had no answers.

"I don't have a choice, so just..." I started before my mom grabbed the phone. They began to have a conversation that I completely tuned out. I was too busy trying to hold myself together in the lobby of this clinic. I felt like if I didn't get this abortion my mama would kick me out. I wouldn't have a place to live. I started crying hard and silently at the same time. I had already been yelled at by a stranger, and two people I cared about wanted me to keep this child. It was too much to handle. This was the lowest point I had ever experienced in my life. She handed me the phone back. My boyfriend and I said "I love you" to each other and hung up the phone.

What seemed like an eternity in the waiting room was over when the nurse called me to the back. They took a sonogram. Then, they took me to another room where I changed into the gown. Waiting in that cold, dimly lit room gave me anxiety like a movie scene when the music changes and you know something bad is about to happen. I had no clue what the process was going to be like or what I would experience.

The doctor came in and told me to lie down on the bed and countdown from 10 to 1. I don't really remember anything after the number 8. When I woke up, the doctor responded "Ok. You can put your clothes on. The nurse will be in shortly." I got dressed and a nurse came in to take me to a recovery room. She told me to just sit in there for a while, but this room was full of women who for one reason or another had done the same thing I had just done. This room was even colder, more silent, and darker than the operating room. It's hard to sit in a room in which there is no space for conversation, no reason to smile, no reason to laugh, and too much shame for even the slightest bit of eye contact.

I sat for a little while and realized that I was starving. I grabbed some cookies and drank some water and then had the sudden urge to throw up. I ran down the hallway to the nearest restroom and those cookies and water came right back up. I was done. I was so over it. I didn't want to sit in that room anymore with all the other women who killed people that day. I told the nurse I was ready to go, and I was not going back into that room. The nurse gave me a birth control shot. Then, she asked if I wanted my sonogram. My mom didn't want it, but I did. I didn't know why I wanted it, but I kept it.

When we left the clinic, I laid in the backseat because my stomach was still hurting. We almost got into a wreck! We were trying to get onto the freeway, but our car slid across all the lanes and went in the opposite way of traffic! I was terrified! I thought God was trying to kill us for killing the baby!

I was convinced from that day that God was very mad at me, I remember saying "See we couldn't even get far away from the place before we almost died." I thought it was a warning of what was to come, and I seriously thought God was done with me. It was hard to live in this false reality that I created. The abortion made me even more depressed than what I had previously been from the things that happened to me as a child. But depression was nothing new to me, so I had to keep on moving through life.

Lifetime Blues

When I was younger, I didn't know what depression was called. I didn't feel special or happy unless someone was giving me attention. I suppressed so many emotions for so many years that it made me confused as to what I was supposed to feel. Throughout junior high and high school, I played sports and was busy with school. There was not a lot of down time to even entertain the thought of being sad. I fed off the energy of the people I was around, so I always needed to be around people to see how I should feel.

I noticed something was wrong with me my freshman year of college. I left everyone I knew August of 2007, and I was excited about going to college. I wasn't excited, however, about a new place and new people. I started to tell myself *I am here for an education. I don't need new friends because I already have some. I am here for an education. I don't need new friends because I already have some*. My freshman year was a mostly lonely one. I only had three friends.

I felt so alone. When I sat in my room alone,

all the emotions I suppressed for years just resurfaced. I felt like I was going to explode. I didn't know what to do with all this. I had no way to numb the pain and hurt. I couldn't have sex because my boyfriend was three hours away, and I couldn't masturbate because I had a roommate. I also didn't have any friends to occupy my time. I was alone and away from every coping mechanism I had ever had.

I got my first F in college in Botany. This was too much for me to handle. I had always been an A/B student. F's didn't exist in my world. I felt like an idiot. I felt like I should not have tried to go to college. I felt like I wasn't smart enough. I absolutely felt lower than the dirt, unworthy, and unimportant. There were so many negative thoughts that entered my mind. All the things I had ever done in my life that made me a failure came rushing back to me like the waves of a tsunami. Failures, mistakes, disappointments all came crashing into the forefront of my mind. I was hopeless at this moment.

My roommate moved out our second semester due to her running track, and the numbing process started again. This left me alone with my thoughts all the time, and it was not good for me. I decided I wanted to die. I sat in my room plenty of days and nights contemplating suicide. I thought about taking a handful of pills. Then I remembered I didn't have any friends, so no one would find me until I was stinky and bloated. That wouldn't be pretty, and my mama wouldn't get to have a nice funeral. So, I thought about jumping off the top of the dorm building, but I knew that wouldn't be pretty. And I might not die, I could just break a bone and still live. I thought about driving into traffic and getting hit head on, but then I thought... *What if I don't die? What if the other people die? What if we both live? What if they die and I don't?!* I didn't want someone else to die because I didn't want to live. I would be killing someone else, and I already knew that feeling wasn't one I wanted because I knew it too well from the abortion.

Looking back now, I know that was God. People who want to die don't have these full conversations about the pros and cons. They just do it. I contemplated everything. I needed a full proof plan that would allow me not to kill anyone else and have an open casket funeral. I never found the "perfect suicide" for me, so I just lived my life every day in despair. I didn't want to be here anymore, but I couldn't find a way to leave.

When the semester ended, I came back to

Fort Worth to people that would reciprocate the love I had for them. This helped me want to live again. The depression did not go away, but I wasn't drowning in darkness anymore. I had many days that were full of light. As I went through life, I heavily dealt with depression. Depression became my comfort zone; it didn't feel right to be happy or joyful. Those emotions felt wrong anytime I would experience them.

When you are in a relationship with depression, it's hard to feel anything opposite of that. I lived in a life of lows with moments of joy and that was the norm for me. Happiness and joy felt uncomfortable to me. I didn't want to feel uncomfortable. My college experience ended, but my depression started to rapidly increase. I would cry all the time except when people were around. I didn't want anybody to know I was feeling like this because I loved Jesus and most of these people looked up to me. I cannot let them see me in this type of emotional stance. I had to be the strong one. I had to be the perfect one.

So, I developed masks to hide my depression from those around me. With my friends, I had to be my strong, encouraging, cool self. With my family, I had to be my happy, loving and selfless self. At work, I had to be my happy, funny, outgoing self. At church I had to be my strong, faith-filled, ready to serve self. My car, however, became my "cry spot." I remember I used to cry all the way until I turned into my church parking lot. Then, I would sit in the car until my eyes were no longer red, get out and proceed with my duties as if nothing was ever wrong.

Church became my other "cry spot". If I cried in church, nobody thought I was depressed. They just thought I was touched by the song or the sermon or God was dealing with me. I rarely had to answer for my tears. I would get a back rub or a hug, and I could just keep crying. It was the perfect cover up for me. I could let out how I was feeling and disguise it as something else. I wanted to be better, but I didn't know where to begin.

I told my first lady one day that I was the fakest person that I know. I was just going through life pretending that all was good, faking strength, but I was so depressed. I was ready to give up. I was crying myself to sleep, waking up crying, crying in the shower, screaming into pillows, and throwing internal fits. I was at my wits end, and I could not fake anymore. No matter what I did to fight depression it always TKO'd me.

Pride's Embarrassment

Water looks like such a calming substance. It is peaceful and tranquil. In large amounts, however, it can sink ships and people. The water in my life came in the form of sex, porn, masturbation, abortion, and depression. I was in deep waters, and I saw nowhere or nothing that could save me from drowning. The only reason I was semi-afloat was due to my relationship with God. It kept me from being completely submerged.

I was finally fed up. I wanted to feel better and be aligned with God's will for my life, so I decided to practice celibacy by the end of 2008. Was I still horny? Yes. Did I still crave the closeness of a body to help me forget life temporarily? Yes. Nonetheless, I still pushed on with my choice. My boyfriend at the time did not like the idea, but he understood my reasoning. I only wish I was as understanding as he was.

Our celibacy usually lasted for about three months. I gave in to the craving to make sure he didn't cheat on me. In my mind, something was better than nothing. I figured I could earn "heaven points" for only having sex sometimes. The only problem was that sex this time felt...well...different. I started to feel some type of guilt after sex. It was a weird anguish that made me feel regret instead of my normal numbness.

When I came back from my spring break vacation in March of 2009, I got a letter from Planned Parenthood that said I had chlamydia. I lost it completely. I was devastated, embarrassed, heart-broken, and confused. Could this really be happening to me? I just felt so nasty like I wasn't worth the gum on the bottom of someone's shoe. I felt cheap and disgusting. The worst part was that I had to go tell the dudes I had slept with through the year to go get tested. It would have been irresponsible to not let them know, so I had to let go of my pride and tell them. That was the most embarrassing thing I have ever had to do in my life.

The Lord knew what it took to get my attention because I had so much pride in the fact that I had never had an STD. I lived for the moments in the club when the DJ would say "All the ladies who ain't never had a STD make some noise!". I wasn't a part of that screaming group of celebratory people anymore. I can't scream and, if I did, I would be lying. On the other hand, it's embarrassing if I don't scream. I took pride in the fact that I maintained good sexual health even though I was reckless sometimes. But I guess it takes a shot to pride for some people to realize God really is trying to make you wake up and pay attention.

The Redemption

Pencils. I used them all through school, but I will admit that I didn't appreciate their abilities. I understand the beauty in pens. They come in different colors and different shapes. Pencils do too. Pencils also give a chance to try again if your first answer or try was not the best or correct. They give you the chance to redeem yourself. A chance to do better than before.

I guess you could call me a reformed pencil if you want. No. I was one of those pencils that looks really pretty on the outside, but it breaks every time you try to write. I had plenty of experience with being broken: broken by molestation, broken by unknowingly molesting others myself, broken from killing my own child, broken from a lifetime of depression, broken from possibly passing a sexually transmitted disease to others. My eraser could never be used. Well...I thought I was useless. It turns out that God is accustomed to broken pencils like me.

He knew why my lead always faltered. He knew the reason for my cheap appearance. He knew, and He still chose me despite all of it. When I realized that He was still around waiting to write a new path with me, I took my celibacy seriously. Every time I slipped up, I always restarted. I always prayed. I consistently continued to fight for Him like He fought for me. And I know His fight for me was not easy.

I thought for the longest that He didn't care. I questioned him a lot. Why would you let these people do this to me? Why would you allow me to hurt others? Why don't You love me like You love others? I know most of us were taught not to question God, but I did. I did it because I saw others doing way better than me. I felt like I was being bullied or ridiculed for absolutely no reason.

One of my biggest questions for God was *Why didn't I have the courage to say something.* My silence didn't just manifest with people. It also manifested in writing. I was so silent about these horrible events that I didn't even write them in my own personal journals. I was traumatized that the one place where I should have been able to express the truth was just as delusional as I was with people. I felt bad for every tear I cried over what happened. They felt like hammers...huge hammers of judgment that I passed on myself. Eventually, I learned from

John 10:10 that all these tactics were actions of the devil. He loves to "steal, kill, and destroy". I knew the kill would come due to the lessons in church I semi-listened to. It was the STEAL and DESTROY that I did NOT see coming. I was expecting Satan to wait and fight fair. He didn't. He stole my innocence and self-image in one foul swoop. I was more concerned with surviving and living when I was young. I didn't think about all the things I lost in my fight to stay alive.

God eventually answered my questions, but it didn't happen in one day. Throughout my path to becoming a better "pencil", I had a lot of moments where I had to sharpen myself with the word of God. When I felt ugly, I remembered Psalm 139:14 *"...I am fearfully and wonderfully made...".* When I would get depressed, I reminded myself of Romans 8:1: *"There is therefore no condemnation for those of us who are in Christ Jesus."* When I wanted to die, He reminded me that I don't have *"...a spirit of fear, but of power and of love, and of a sound mind."* When I had sexual desires or I felt guilty because I fell off track, I sharpened myself with Colossians 1: 21-22: *"And you, who were alienated and hostile in mind, doing evil deeds, he has now reconciled in his body of flesh by his death, in order to present you holy and blameless and above reproach to God through Jesus."* I am

Holy. I am not to be condemned and I am above disappointing him. When I felt worthless, He allowed John 3:16 to remind me that His ultimate sacrifice was for me...faults and all.

The pencil I am now is grateful for all the breaking points, stops and restarts, and even the sharpening moments. I never thought in my life that I would be free from masturbation and porn. I have been celibate for a little over seven years. I forgave those in my past for their actions. It wasn't easy, but I am here. God answers your prayers in His time, and His time is exactly when it is needed. Is it a process? Yes. I spent more time at altars and in prayer than anyone I know. However, He never gave up on my deliverance. He never gave up on my redemption. Never give up on your deliverance, you have been REDEEMED!

The Recovery in Progress

When I realized redemption was possible even for me, it changed the way I viewed myself. I started seeing myself as a child that God loves completely. Getting your spirit lined up with God is more important than looking the part of change. Once your inner appearance is changed, your outer appearance will fall right in line. I am not just saying this. I know this because I have been in recovery for years.

Recovery is not always fun, but it is very important to the healing process. Think of it as the post-op of a big surgery. You are in the recovery room. Your surgery went well, but you are not able to use your body at its full ability yet. In the next coming days, you are released from the hospital, but you still have some limitations.

It's just like this for me in my Christ Centered Recovery Journey. I intentionally separated myself from triggers that will pull me back to that thing that God just removed in surgery. I had to forgive people...even if they never asked for forgiveness. I had to distance myself from people and places for a while. Some of those people and places were permanently banned from my post-op life. This was hard for me because most of my identity was based on them. I had to really ask myself: WHO AM I? It took a while, but I eventually became me: unapologetically, authentically, and amazingly. I found my identity in Christ, and I'm finally loving the me I see.

As I continue my recovery process, I want to share with you some things that helped me make it through. This is not a formula for freedom or a set checklist of what to do. Everyone's process will be different. You may choose to keep some of what I did. You may choose not to. Either way, my prayer for you is that you find a process that works best for you and your walk with Christ.

Cold Turkey

One of the hardest parts of my recovery was eliminating masturbation from my life. I started about 2 ½ years into my celibacy to wean myself off the habit. I moved in with two roommates, and I deliberately chose the loft room to stay so I would have no privacy at all. It had no door, and it was opened to the living room downstairs. If I was bored, I talked to my roommates, watched TV, or went and exercised. I kept my mind occupied and distracted. Sometimes it worked, and sometimes I gave in. If I gave in, I always repented and asked God to help me gain self-control so I can please Him with my body.

I watched a spoken word video on YouTube by Ezekiel Azonwu called "Touchy Subject". My eyes were completely opened. This video helped me start down the road to stopping masturbation. You will not believe how many bumps, potholes, construction hazards, and detours existed on this road! It was not an instant change, but I improved every day.

1 Corinthians 10:13 (ESV) says that "No temptation has overtaken you that is not common to man. God is faithful, and He will not let you be tempted beyond your ability, but with the temptation he will also provide the way of escape, that you may be able to endure it." What we experience when trying to move forward is not new. It is going to be hard. It is going to be arduous. But if we stay consistent with going back to God for help, we can move forward.

Spoken Word

I got really into spoken word at the start of my recovery, and I still love it to this day. I listened to Preston Perry and Itohan Omolere spit a poem called "Soul Ties". It completely wrecked me. The poem was about breaking off relationships that are not pleasing to God and not letting flesh make your life decisions. Instead, you should allow God to fill the voids and to be ENOUGH for you.

I never really thought about soul ties in that manner before. I stopped doing a lot of stuff, cut off a lot of people, and didn't go to a lot of places anymore. However, they still had my heart. My desire was still to reconnect with those people and still be able to hang out in those places. I had to pray for God to break every soul tie I had attached to me regardless if it was human or an idea.

I also listened to a woman named Janette Ikz spit a poem called "The Truth Without Photoshop". It's about not photoshopping the truth so that her testimony will look more appealing and comfortable to the world. She talked very boldly and honestly about what she experienced in her life and how it affected her.

These artists told their testimonies so honestly and boldly that it encouraged me. They stood on a stage with cameras on them and told the world what they had been through and about the God who keeps them and frees them. I hid those poems in my heart for a very long time. I listened to them daily because they were my inspirations. If God had set them free, I knew He could do the same for me. And He did. Now that I am free, I still listen to them when I need some encouragement. Those pieces of artistry helped immensely when God was calling me to write a book where I had to be open and honest. Like them, my story in this book is exposed to people I know and don't know.

Deuteronomy 31:6 (ESV) says to "Be strong and courageous. Do not fear or be in dread of them, for it is the Lord your God who goes with you. He will not leave you or forsake you." Going through recovery is already difficult by itself. Take the time to find inspiration to help you stay strong and stay courageous. Spoken word helped me. What can help you? Reading? Watching inspiration videos? Listening to an inspirational podcast? Find your "picker upper" you can go to when all seems lost. I pray that this book does for you what those poems did for me because they truly changed my life.

(Side Note: Preston Perry has another video called "Necrophiliac" that gives his testimony telling what got him in the situation to have soul ties and his experiences. Check that one out as well.)

Routine Changes

To stay in recovery, I had to change some of the things that I was used to doing, seeing, and listening to. Some people think I am extreme, but I must do whatever it takes to keep my mind and body pure. I do my best to protect my ears and eyes from anything that I believe will cause me to miss my sexual sin.

I don't listen to music with very sexual context or old songs that were on the "slow jam" cd. (The CD back in the day that had all the get in the right mood songs on it.) Yeah...they had to go. I don't watch sex scenes in movies or tv shows. Period. If I am at a theatre, I act like I'm 3 years old. I close my eyes and my ears until that part is over. I will unblock my ears to see if it sounds over so I can continue watching the movie. If I am at home, I fast forward the part or change the channel until the scene is over. I do this because I know it can take only one memory trigger or visual to revert my mind back to the thinking it had practiced for over half of my life.

I was at the movies with my mama one time, and a sex scene came on. I covered my ears and eyes. She laughed so hard at me and was mocking me in a sense. After the movie, I had to explain to her that I used to be addicted to porn. Sometimes, movies have very explicit pornographic type scenes, and I don't want to do anything to tempt my flesh. That was not an easy conversation to have, but it was necessary. In the end, it helped her understand me a little better.

2 Corinthians 5:17 declares that "... if anyone is in Christ, he is a new creation. The old has died; behold, the new has come." Rolling with Christ means a new routine. I am not saying you must give up your entire life, but you can't do the things that caused you to require the surgery. You must do whatever it takes to protect yourself, even if other people laugh or don't understand. Remember, it's YOUR conviction. Not theirs. You must make up your mind about what you are going to accept and what you will not and stick to it. For me, I am not watching or listening to the sex scenes, period. What is your routine change?

Choose Your Village Wisely

First Lady A'Besa Hodge always says that "If it don't fit, don't force it." As an extrovert, I want everyone to fit. I like to enjoy the company of people. The recovery, however, required me to surround myself with people who do not put me in situations to be tempted. So, I had to choose my village very carefully. I had to intentionally make those connections with like-minded people and people who would understand my journey. I didn't cut off every person that doesn't agree with my lifestyle, but they don't have full access to me like before. I know how to dismiss myself from any situations or atmospheres that do not compliment my journey.

I thank God for the people I have around me because they don't put me in situations that would allow me to be tempted. I love my best friend Ashley because she is the only person who will change the music in her car when she is driving if a song comes on that she knows is extremely sexual. She has never once made me feel like it's inconvenient for her to do so. 98% of the time she catches them before I do and turns the song off. I truly appreciate God for her because there are few people in this world that I have come across that will put someone's salvation before their own preferences. I have so many people in my life now that support me and are striving for me to do great in my recovery journey.

Matthew 7:13-14 (ESV) states to "Enter by the narrow gate. For the gate is wide and the way is easy that leads to destruction, and those who enter by it are many. For the gate is narrow and the way is hard that leads to life, and those who find it are few." This passage reminds me that it is ok if my village is not big and full of people. Those who are there have meaning. They have value. You may have to dismiss yourself from people that could potentially get you caught up. Check the people around you and make sure they are truly for you. If you want to change and the people you hang around are not on the same page, it is time for a seasonal or permanent separation. Everybody is not going to agree with your change, especially if they are not trying to change. Nonetheless, you must surround yourself with a group of people who are for you and want you to grow. That might mean you and your best friend since 3rd grade are not going to be talking for a while. Who is your village? Who helps you to think better and do better?

Set Realistic Boundaries

Being in my 30s, single and celibate there are many challenges I have faced. I have been told many times that I need to do "some stuff" and I could keep a man, but I beg to differ. There is nothing in my Bible that declares I should put the standards of the world over what God asks of me. It tells me in 1 Peter 2:11 "Beloved, I urge you as sojourners and exiles to abstain from the passions of the flesh, which wage war against your soul." So, doing "some stuff" is waging war against my soul. I have enough forces fighting against me. I don't need to be at war with myself.

So even in dating I have set myself up some boundaries so that I don't find myself in a situation that will start my celibacy journey over. It's not a common thing in today's time and especially not with my generation. I take my recovery very seriously because I know the life I used to live and how empty it was. I never want to go back there.

Psalm16: 5-9 (ESV) explains that "The Lord is my chosen portion and my cup; you hold my lot. The lines have fallen for me in pleasant places; indeed, I have a beautiful inheritance. I bless the Lord who gives me counsel; in the night also, my heart instructs me. I have set the Lord always before me; because he is at my right hand, I shall not be shaken. Therefore, my heart is glad, and my whole being rejoices; my flesh also dwells secure." In other words, boundaries with God create healthy boundaries for your life. When you make the choice to allow God to lead your life, people are going to have things to say, but God's opinion about you is THE ONLY one that matters. People don't have a heaven or hell to put me in, so trying to please them is not my life goal. What are you willing or not willing to do? What is going to help you continue a healthy relationship with God?

Counseling AND GOD

During my recovery, it took a lot for me to realize that I needed professional help. I needed someone who knows God and has a degree that qualifies them to give guidance to my mental state. I went to counseling in 2017 for about six months, and it changed my life. I was able to discover some things about myself that I didn't realize I was even dealing with. Counseling gave me the opportunity to be completely truthful for the first time ever. Every emotion I felt, I spoke it. Every thought I had, I said it without judgement. I would always joke with my counselor about me going to need to replenish her tissue collection because I went through so many each session. But it was so cleansing to my soul and it allowed me to begin the healing process in a lot of areas in my life.

It took talking to God, reading God's word, counseling, my community of believers, and a lot of prayer to get me where I am and keep me where I am today. My recovery process has been a myriad of different avenues, but it's working for me.

I can see the truth in Psalm 119:71 that says, "It is good for me that I was afflicted, that I might learn your statutes." In your process to recovery, it helps to process and understand your hurt and pain through counseling. This doesn't mean you think God is bad at His job of healing you. Instead, it means you are willing to work toward your mental and spiritual improvement. Do not let stigmas or stereotypes keep you from fully healing from your surgery. What do you need to deal with mentally and emotionally? What do you need to talk about so you can "let go and let God have His way"?

I can admit now that I'm grateful for every single amount of deliverance from myself by God. I would not have been a great mom. I would not have been a great wife. I needed to get a STD. I would have seriously damaged my own life and the lives of others, but God knew what He was doing. He knew I couldn't get to Him on my own. I needed a serious wake up call, and it wasn't going to come until I had to come to terms with myself and my decisions.

If I'm honest, I always treated God like I treated people. I didn't let Him into the deep parts of my soul or too far into my emotions. Contemplating suicide was a way for God to show me that He is the author and finisher. All my pain was worth my promise. I would not change a single moment of what I went through. It has broken me gracefully, and it built me up to be better.

Some people know bits and pieces of my testimony. It still amazes me how so many people have been through something similar, or they are experiencing the same now. The devil will try to keep you silent. He will whisper to you "People don't want to hear that!" or "You should be ashamed you went through that!" or "What happens in the family...stays in your family." I believed those lies for the longest time.

I felt like I couldn't write this book until I was delivered from my sin of masturbation. Thankfully, I was freed from it in the midst of writing this book. Please... Please... Please know... You are NOT ALONE. Peter 5:9 reminds us to stay firm in our faith and know that others like us are experiencing the same suffering.

The Bible tells us we are never alone. Ever. There are many scriptures that confirm we are made for the community. We were created to help, encourage, uplift, listen, worship, and rejoice together. God is very strategic. Words have power. It's like once you have heard that someone else has survived that, you have a living example for yourself. You can make it out too! Don't be stifled by embarrassment or horror if God wants you to supply a testimony. Someone really needs it.

The storm was ugly and treacherous. I didn't think I could survive. Nonetheless, I am here. You will make it too. God called me to be UNCOVERED in this season. While I didn't want to accept the challenge, His plan was bigger than my wants. It was His need for me. I pray that through this transparency you are drawn closer to the Lord and led towards COMPLETE deliverance and freedom.

It's Your Turn

I live my life now uncovered, and I am so grateful for the new opportunities God has given me. Now, I want you to have the same opportunities. Tell me your story. You can choose to share it or not. This book will hold on to your words until you are ready to live your life uncovered too.

_____

_____

_____

_____

_____

_____

_____

_____

Uncovered

Kee'Twana Williams

_____

_____

_____

_____

_____

_____

_____

_____

_____

_____

_____

_____

_____

Get Connected

 Facebook.com/KeeTwanaWilliams

 Instagram.com/keekee_blessed

Kee'Twana Williams